The Ultimate Self-Teaching Method! Level Two

Play Drums Today!

by Scott Schroedl and Doug Downing

A Complete Guide to the Basics

Contents

 Introduction

Track 1

Welcome to Level 2 of *Play Drums Today!*, the series designed to prepare you for any style of drumming. Whatever your taste in music—rock, blues, jazz, R&B, country, funk, Latin—*Play Drums Today!* will give you the start you need.

In Level 1, we covered the basics of music and of the drums. In Level 2, we'll really expand on that knowledge. We'll explore many different styles of music and even some new techniques to improve your overall drumming "chops." Many of the beats and techniques will cross over into various styles, so practice them all!

To better understand the different styles represented in this book, listen to the audio track for each example before trying to play it. This will ensure that you get the correct "feel." (As always, you'll be accompanied by a band on almost every song, making learning to play easier and more enjoyable.) Many of the examples on the audio may be difficult to keep up with at first—if that's the case, practice them slowly on your own for a while, and gradually speed them up as you become more confident. Then, when you're ready, play along and have fun!

Recording credits:

Todd Greene, Producer
Jake Johnson, Engineer
Doug Boduch, Guitar
Scott Schroedl, Drums

Tom McGirr, Bass
Warren Wiegratz, Keyboards
Michael Landers, Narration

To access audio visit:
www.halleonard.com/mylibrary

Enter Code
5193-6705-4084-8265

ISBN 978-1-5400-5236-0

Your Drumkit

Set 'Em Up

Just a reminder: Here's what a typical "five-piece" drumkit looks like. Arrange your own kit similarly. We'll add a few extras as we proceed in the book.

Ride cymbal   Tom-toms   Crash cymbal

Hi-hat

Snare drum

Floor tom   Bass drum

Read 'Em

Of course, you need to be able to recognize these drums and cymbals on the staff, so here's a quick review. (If you made it through Level 1, you should be well-practiced!)

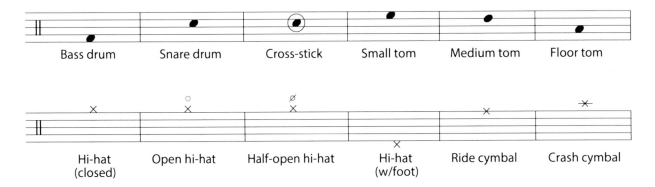

Bass drum   Snare drum   Cross-stick   Small tom   Medium tom   Floor tom

Hi-hat (closed)   Open hi-hat   Half-open hi-hat   Hi-hat (w/foot)   Ride cymbal   Crash cymbal

Get In Rhythm!

Rhythm refers to how long, or how many beats, a note lasts. This is indicated with the following symbols:

Whole note	Half note	Quarter note	Eighth note	Sixteenth note	Dotted quarter note	Dotted eighth note
(4 beats)	(2 beats)	(1 beat)	(1/2 beat)	(1/4 beats)	(1 1/2 beats)	(3/4 beat)

Silences, or rests, are notated similarly:

Whole	Half	Quarter	Eighth	Sixteenth	Dotted quarter	Dotted eighth

To help you keep track of the beat, songs are divided into measures. A *time signature* at the beginning of the staff indicates how many beats you can expect to find in each measure.

time signature

top number $\longrightarrow$ 4 = number of beats per measure
bottom number $\longrightarrow$ 4 = type of note that receives one beat

3
4   3 beats per measure
quarter note (1/4) gets one beat

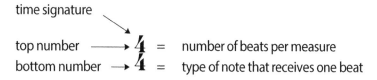

count: 1   2   3   1   2   3

4
4   4 beats per measure
4 quarter note (1/4) gets one beat

count: 1   2   3   4   1   2   3   4

Triplets

If a beat is divided into three, you'll see a *triplet*.

count: 1 - trip - let   2 - trip - let   3 - trip - let   4 - trip - let

Triplets are three notes played evenly in the time normally taken by two notes. Triplets create a unique feel and are the basis of "shuffle" rhythm.

Warm-Up

The purpose of this section is to review some techniques and to warm up your hands and feet before you start practicing. Use this routine every time you sit down to play, before continuing with wherever you left off in the book.

Let's begin with a snare warm-up to get your hands moving from slow to fast, back to slow again.

Now play alternating sixteenth notes on the snare, and accent the notes marked.

Try rim shots on the snare to create a sharper attack sound. Play with the right stick for the first two measures; then with the left stick for the next two.

Flip your left stick around and play the cross-stick sound on beats 2 and 4.

Starting on the snare, alternate hands around the toms.

4

Play flams (hit one stick softer just before the other) on the snare and toms with the bass drum coordinated in between.

While keeping constant eighth notes going on the ride, practice alternating your feet and playing them together.

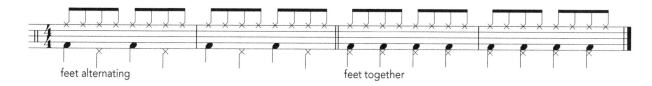

feet alternating   feet together

The ride cymbal produces different sounds when played on the bell and on the shoulder.

shoulder of ride   bell of ride

Practice getting from the crash back to the ride smoothly, and end with an abrupt cymbal choke.

choke

Explore the different sounds possible on the hi-hat including closed, half-open, and open.

closed hats   half-open hats   open hats

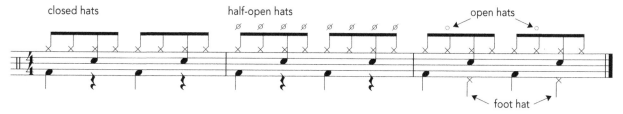

foot hat

Get your hands working between the hi-hat and snare.

R L R L R L R L R L R L R L R L

Rock 'n' Roll

Rock 'n' roll began in the '50s and drew from a variety of styles: mainly blues, R&B, and country—but also gospel, jazz, and folk. Some of its early pioneers included Chuck Berry, Elvis Presley, Little Richard, Jerry Lee Lewis, Buddy Holly, Bo Diddley, Bill Haley, the Everly Brothers, and Carl Perkins.

Straight Eighth-Note Rock

Let's begin with some straight eighth-note rock 'n' roll.

This is a fairly easy beat, and it sounds great. Just make sure to play the quarter-note snare and bass drum notes exactly together with the ride cymbal.

Track 3

All Four Rock

► Notice the double snare hits on beat 4 of every other measure.

In some ways, these next two beats are even easier, but you may need to practice the bass and snare drum parts to get comfortable with them.

Track 4

Drivin'

Track 5

I Wonder

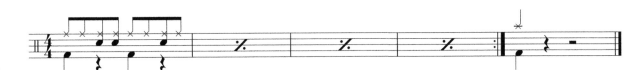

One and Two-Measure Repeats

REMINDER: The symbol ∕ means to repeat the previous measure. A similar sign ∕∕ is used to indicate a two-measure repeat.

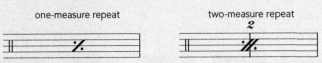

This groove is similar to "I Wonder" except that you're playing the mid tom. Watch that bass drum pattern, too.

Track 6

Two And

Now try this up-tempo rocker. Switching from eighth notes to quarter notes on the ride changes the feel on the second line.

Track 7

► Practice this one slowly at first. The sixteenth-note fills can be a challenge.

Faster Now

Shuffle-Based Rock

Much of the drumming on early rock 'n' roll records was based on the triplet feel; this is because many of the drummers playing this music were originally "swing" drummers. As you'll recall, the basic shuffle (a.k.a. "swing") rhythm is obtained by leaving out the middle note of a three-note triplet group:

"Brown Shoes" is based on the shuffle rhythm played on the half-open hi-hat. The hi-hats should sound loose or "sloshy."

Brown Shoes

Track 8

► Again, practice these slowly at first, to get the shuffle feel.

For "Hot Dog," make sure that the second bass drum note is played in time with the ride cymbal. This can be tricky.

Hot Dog

Track 9

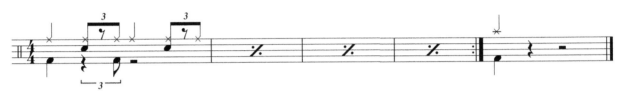

Try using this combination of tom-toms for "Susie Who?" Notice that the rhythm is similar to the last example, and yet it sounds quite different. The low tom carries the shuffle on beat 4.

Susie Who?

Track 10

You may find some of these beats difficult at first. If that's the case, and you get frustrated, take a break—or move on, and then come back to them later. Some things take time to process. When you return, you may be surprised to find that they've become a lot easier for you. (If not, just keep practicing!)

Occasionally in early rock 'n' roll, the drummer actually shuffles while the rest of the band plays straight eighth notes. Sound odd? Listen carefully to the next example, "Rollin' Train."

Rollin' Train

Track 11

The Shuffle Indication ()

Shuffle notation can be hard to read. So instead, you'll often see shuffle or swing grooves written as straight eighth notes with the word "swing" or () written at the beginning of the music. This tells you to play all eighth notes with a shuffle feel.

Although they look different, both of the above examples would be played exactly the same. You can think of the sound as: "long-short, long-short, long-short, long-short."

Try "Places to Go." The snare drum is playing the shuffle rhythm with the left hand. Remember to play the accented notes louder.

Track 12

Places to Go

Breaking It Down

On challenging grooves, you may find it helpful to break the parts down and build your coordination gradually. For example, on "Places to Go," you could start with the snare and bass drum parts. Next, add a quarter-note ride cymbal (keep things simple at first). Then add the foot hi-hat on beats 2 and 4.

Now try the actual ride part with the snare. Then, add the foot hi-hat (adding the accents in the hands will help you get in sync). Finally, put everything together!

The Clave

Here's a fun beat in the style that Bo Diddley's drummer played in the '50s. It's based on a Latin pattern called a *clave*:

count: **1** & 2 **&** 3 & **4** & 1 & **2** & **3** & 4 &

Try this with a straight eighth-note feel, as notated, and then try shuffling it.

Here's the shuffled version. The bass drum reinforces the clave pattern. The accents are everything!

Track 13

Shufflin' Floor Tom

Surf Rock

Surf rock began in the early '60s with reverb-drenched guitars played by artists like Dick Dale and the Surfaris. Later, bands like the Beach Boys and Jan & Dean added their original pop harmonies to further define this sound. The beat for this is typically driving, straight eighth-note-based.

Here's a fast one with a short snare fill every fourth measure. Remember four-bar phrasing?

Track 14

Wave Rider

▶ Be sure to play this one straight, *not* shuffled.

Four-Bar Phrases

Many songs are based on four-bar phrases. As a drummer, that means you'll typically lay down a groove for about three measures or so, and then add an improvised fill:

The fill literally "fills in the gap" at the end of the phrase or section. A cymbal crash is often added to highlight the start of the next phrase.

Sticking Principles

Hopefully, you noticed the "sticking" indications (e.g., RLRL) on some of the previous fills. These are included to help clear up any confusion you might have about how to play them. Good sticking is designed to help you play cleanly and easily—and to get you moving around the drums more quickly.

Let's practice our sticking with a few fills using just the snare drum. First, imagine you're playing alternating sixteenth notes beginning with your right stick:

Now, for these next fills, keep that same sticking pattern (RLRL); however, if a note is skipped, so is its corresponding hand. You can try "air drumming" these hands if you like (play in the air, but don't hit anything) to keep the alternating sixteenths flowing, or not. This may seem awkward at first, but if you understand the principle, your drumming will be greatly enhanced:

The exception to the above "alternating sixteenths" rule is when playing consecutive eighth notes in a fill. Just alternate hands for the eighths, and then go back to alternating sixteenths:

Are you wondering why all of these fills lead with the right hand? Most fills are played around the toms from left to right, and leading with the right hand helps eliminate your sticks from crossing over. Don't be afraid to experiment on your own. Practice also leading with your left hand. Remember: when mixing up your fills between the snare and toms in a different order, they will require different stickings. Practice them until you find the most logical order.

To close this lesson, let's try a short rock 'n' roll song. This one starts with a drum fill on beat 3 of the pickup measure. On the track, you'll hear one full measure of count-off ("1, 2, 3, 4"), then two more clicks for the pickup measure ("1, 2"), and then you enter with the fill.

By the way, be sure to choke the crash cymbal at the end, for an abrupt finish.

Rockin' '50s

1st and 2nd Endings

You'll notice the above song has a **1st and 2nd ending** (indicated by brackets and the numbers "1" and "2"). The first time through the song, you should play the 1st ending, up until the repeat sign (:‖) and then return to the initial repeat at the beginning of the song. The second time through, skip the 1st ending and jump to the 2nd ending, playing until the end of the song.

Country

Early country didn't include drums when it went commercial with its first record in the mid '20s; drums came into play much later—in the '50s. Of course, country music as we know it today commonly includes drums along with fiddle, banjo, dobro, steel guitar, acoustic and electric guitar, bass, harmonica, and mandolin.

Classic Country

Let's begin with some "classic country" beats. These are still used today on many recordings. The first is a two-beat feel with the accents on the "ands."

Track 16

Two Beat #1

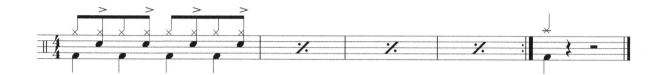

Now try a variation of the two-beat feel.

Track 17

Two Beat #2

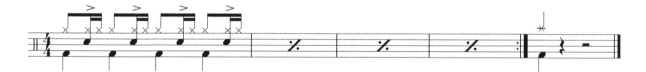

Cut Time and the "Two-Beat" Feel

The two-beat feel gets its name because it's actually felt in *cut time*, or *2/2*, in which there are two beats in each measure. Here's how "Two-Beat #1" and "Two-Beat #2" would look in 2/2 time:

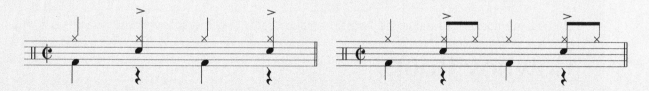

As you can see, in 2/2, the bass drum is played twice in each measure—once for each beat, or half note. This is where the bassist usually plays as well, accentuating the feel.

The "train beat" is named for its locomotive sound. It's played with alternating hands on the snare drum using sticks, brushes, or multi-rods. Play the unaccented snare notes much softer than the accented. This may take some practice to get the dynamics and the speed.

Track 18

Steam Engine

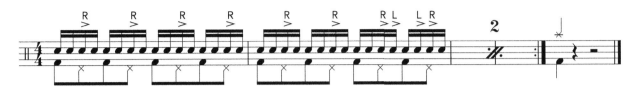

Brushes and Multi-Rods

Brushes and multi-rods are two popular alternatives to drumsticks that can add color to your playing. *Brushes* are much quieter than sticks and are typically used to vary the snare sound when playing country or jazz. The brush wires can also be dragged across the snare head, for a "stir" effect (this is why many snare heads have a white textured coating). *Multi-rods* also have a unique sound—louder than brushes but quieter than sticks. Made up of small wooden dowels wrapped together, multi-rods produce a loose, slapping sound.

This is another version of the train beat—this time, utilizing the shuffle. This is fun to play at all tempos. Once again, alternate your hands.

Track 19

Shufflin' Snare

This is a more jazz-like beat in the "western swing" style. Play the accents heavy on beats 2 and 4.

Track 20

Cowboy Boots

► Listen to the bassist's "walking line" on this track.

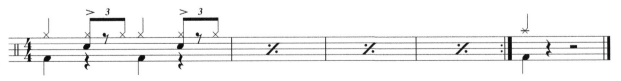

Many country tunes are in 3/4 time—usually referred to as a **waltz.** Try the next two examples using the cross-stick sound. The first is played straight, and the second is shuffled. Both of these are on the same track so you can hear the difference between the two feels.

Gone To Texas

Lazy River

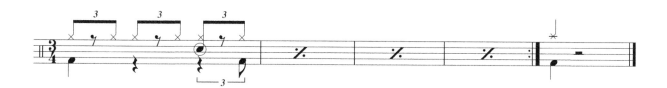

We promised you some fills for 3/4 time back in Lesson 13. So here they are—four with a straight eighth-note feel, and four with a shuffle feel. Once you've got these down, try inserting them into the fourth measure of each groove above, or into other 3/4 grooves.

3/4 Fills

Contemporary Country

Contemporary country songs often favor a straight eighth-note feel, much like pop music.

In the Pocket

Track 23

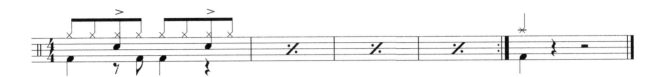

This beat is nice for a slower country ballad, again using the cross-stick.

Leaving Home

Track 24

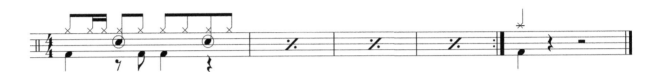

Contemporary country also uses the shuffle feel from time to time. Try these two variations at a moderate tempo.

Rural Route

Track 25

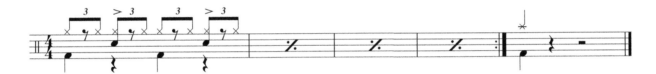

Cheatin'

"Ghost Town" is a shuffle ballad.

Ghost Town

Track 26

"Country Rock" uses cross-stick and tambourine for some textural variety. If you don't have a tambourine on your kit, just use cross-stick on the snare throughout.

Country Rock

► The guitars on this track give the song a "rock" sound.

Intro

Chorus

Verse

Chorus

Tambourine

Drumset tambourine differs from hand-held tambourine because it's fitted with a special clamp to mount to your drums or cymbal stands. It can be placed anywhere on your drumset. Most commonly, tambourine is used as a substitute for snare hits on beats 2 and 4 in quieter passages, or to replace the hi-hat pattern for a different texture. Typically, it's played with a drumstick, but, for a softer attack, you can also hit it with your hand. Try adding tambourine to some beats you already know just for fun.

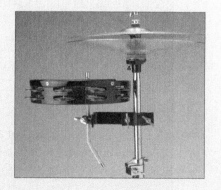

R&B

The original meaning of R&B was "rhythm and blues"—a form of music that evolved in the '40s, characterized by heavily syncopated dance rhythms and the use of blues scales. Later, R&B became a broader term for popular music that combined elements of blues, jazz, and rock 'n' roll.

Gospel

Gospel is a form of religious or inspirational music often played in an R&B style. Let's begin with a fun gospel groove played on the snare drum. Use alternate sticking, and be sure to accent beats 2 and 4. The hi-hat with foot consistently keeps time, but notice how the bass drum plays "off the beat" in measure 2. As always, begin slowly and speed up when you get the hang of it.

Track 28

Gospel Beat #1

This time, the right hand plays quarter notes on the hi-hat, and the left plays backbeats on the snare, again accenting beats 2 and 4. The bass drum plays the same part as in the previous example.

Track 29

Gospel Beat #2

If this groove gives you trouble, it's probably in the second measure. Try looping that measure—playing it over and over—very slowly, until you can play it continuously. Go as slow as you have to, just to get the movements down. Then try speeding it up. Finally, go back and try the whole groove again.

Syncopation

Playing "off the beat" is a way of adding rhythmic interest to a groove. The musical term for this is **syncopation**. It means "putting a strong note on a weak beat"—for example, playing or accenting the upbeats (the "ands") instead of the downbeats ("1," "2," "3," or "4").

Of course, we've been playing syncopated grooves for a while—we just didn't have a name for it yet!

Soul

Soul is another type of R&B—typically smoother, slicker, and a bit more commercial than pure rhythm 'n' blues. On the other hand, sometimes it can be gritty, too.

This one uses a popular bass drum pattern.

 Track 30

The Standard

▶ Notice the open hi-hat before the repeat.

"Soulful" is a mid-tempo soul groove that uses **ghost notes**. These are notes that are barely played, but add quite a bit to the feel. The ghost notes appear in parentheses; play them softly. If you find it difficult to play them softly, then play them normally at first. Then work on ghosting them.

 Track 31

Soulful

Here's a more relaxing triplet groove.

 Track 32

Triplet Hat

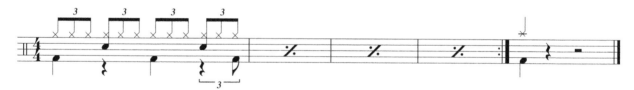

The combination of open and closed hi-hat with the syncopated bass drum makes this one a challenge.

 Track 33

Moderate R&B

Motown

The Motown sound—a bright, pop-oriented version of R&B—emanated in the '60s and '70s from the Detroit-based Motown Records. The name Motown was derived from the words "motor" and "town," a nickname for Detroit, which was a hub of the auto manufacturing industry. The sound consists of a strong backbeat, bouncy bass lines, and soulful vocals.

Track 34

Hat Shuffle

▶ Observe the shuffle indication on this groove.

"Sweet Sugar" uses a quarter-note pulse on the snare drum. This is a very popular Motown groove.

Track 35

Sweet Sugar

Listen to how the bass guitar follows the bass drum part in "Sunshine."

Track 36

Sunshine

Locking In

"Locking in" means listening to what the bassist is playing and being aware of how the bass and the drums work together to create a total groove. In fact, it's a good idea to have some concept of what the bass is playing—often, it will follow your bass drum pattern, or vice versa:

Offbeat Bass

The Sixteenth-Note Shuffle

Remember shuffled eighth notes? Sixteenth notes can be shuffled, too. The underlying feel is triplet-based:

sixteenth-note
triplets

sixteenth-note
shuffle

Like the eighth-note shuffle, sixteenth-note shuffles are often written straight with a shuffle indication appearing at the beginning of the music.

"Emotional" uses shuffled sixteenth notes. Listen to the track before playing. (Keep in mind, only the sixteenths are shuffled; the eighths are straight.)

Emotional

Let's continue with the shuffled sixteenth feel on another short song. This song also includes ghost notes on the snare. It begins with a pickup fill; you'll hear three "clicks," then begin playing.

The Preacher

Track 39

▶ Notice the switch from the hi-hat to the ride, which changes the feel of each section.

Jazz and Blues

Jazz has been around for over 100 years. There are many different types of jazz, so we'll just touch on some of the basics to give you a better understanding of the general style.

For starters, you should know that the ride cymbal and hi-hat are the basis of timekeeping when playing jazz. The foot hat is typically used to accent beats 2 and 4, while the ride or hi-hat with stick play a shuffle pattern.

Swing

Swing is one of the original styles of jazz that caught on in the mid '30s with big bands such as Duke Ellington, Benny Goodman, and Count Basie.

Sometimes, all you need to play to hold the whole band together is the hi-hat. How about trying that right now?

Track 40

Swingin'

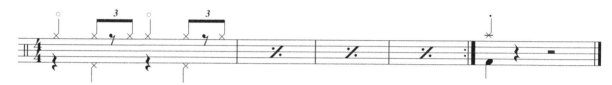

Try this one on the ride cymbal with your right hand, and play a cross-stick on beat 4 with your left hand.

Track 41

Playing Time

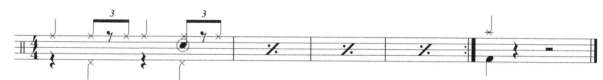

Next, let's add the snare and bass drum. These are played considerably softer than the cymbals in jazz or swing—especially in comparison to, say, rock 'n' roll—unless you're accenting certain musical phrases with the band.

Track 42

► Jazz is based around the quarter-note pulse.

Basic Jazz

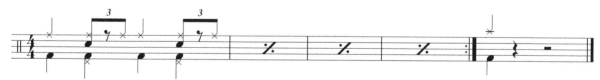

Quarter notes on the ride and with occasional swinging triplets are an effective approach to establishing the quarter-note pulse of jazz. "Broken Up" will give you an idea of this concept.

Track 43

Broken Up

Improvisation

Jazz is an improvisational type of music—players compose "on the spot" around standard melodies or themes. When playing in a band situation, you would embellish upon these basic grooves by interacting with the other players spontaneously.

Try "Jazzy." This is how a typical improvised jazz drum part might look if written out.

Jazzy

► Notice how the snare is played casually, off the beat, in the melody section.

For more ideas on improvisation, go back to the snare coordination exercises in Lesson 12. These are a great way of developing your improvisational chops.

Rumba Boogie

Another fun jazz beat is the rumba boogie. This uses the cross-stick sound with the left hand, while the right hand plays normally. So, flip around your left stick for the cross-stick sound (play the tom using the butt end of the left stick) and follow the sticking indicated. This one begins with a sixteenth-note triplet starting on the "and" of beat 1. The real difficulty lies in getting from the cross-stick on the snare to the tom and back to the cross-stick smoothly.

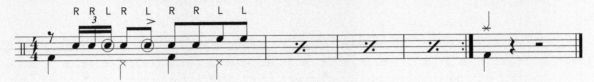

For a full-set rumba that's less complex, try this next pattern. By the way, both of these rumba beats are played straight, not swung.

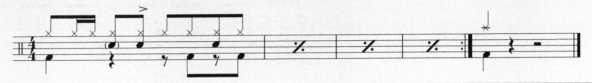

Blues

Blues evolved in the deep South from the spirituals and work songs of African-Americans in the early 1900s. Over the years, the blues branched out into many different sub-types that have their very own distinctions. We'll just touch on the basics here to get you started.

Part of what makes blues unique is its predictable structure—most commonly, blues songs follow what's called a *12-bar form**. This doesn't mean that a song is only 12 bars (or measures) long, but rather, that it's based on a 12-bar chord progression, which repeats:

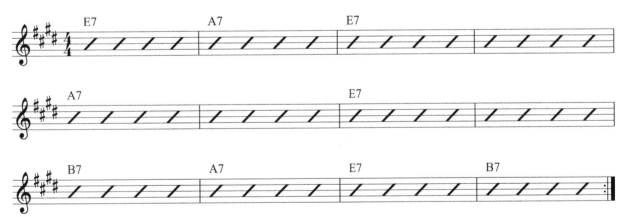

As a drummer, you don't need to know what chords are being played, but you should be able to hear the changes as they occur. Most importantly, you should realize that the 12-bar form consists of three four-bar phrases. (Look at the example above again if you didn't see this.) While you wouldn't likely insert a fill at the end of every four-bar phrase in a blues tune, you might choose to highlight the beginning of some phrases with a cymbal crash, and use a fill to mark the end of a 12-bar section.

* The 12-bar form is used in other styles as well. In fact, you've already played this as a rock 'n' roll progression in Lesson 1—remember "Rockin' '50s"?

Let's try some popular blues grooves in the shuffle style. These all use the 12-bar form. Listen to the audio to hear the progression.

Track 46

Basic Shuffle

12/8 Time

Until now, you've been playing shuffle or swing grooves in 4/4 time. Another way they can be written, however, particularly slow ones, is in **12/8** time. In 12/8, there are twelve beats (or counts) per measure, and the eighth note receives one beat.

count:　**1**　2　3,　**4**　5　6,　**7**　8　9,　**10**　11　12

Notice above that the eighth notes are grouped into threes—much like triplets. That's because the underlying pulse is actually a dotted quarter note; beats 1, 4, 7, and 10—the first note of each three-note group—are accented. For example, compare the following two beats: One is written as triplets in 4/4, the other as eighth notes in 12/8. (They both sound the same.)

Eighth notes in the hi-hat plus a very active shuffle pattern in the kick drum give this 12/8 beat a very distinctive feel. Take it slow.

Slow Blues

Now the shuffle pattern is on the ride. Add snare hits on the "and" of each quarter note and a four-to-the-bar kick drum pattern with foot hat on beats 2 and 4, and you've got a challenging, but unique upbeat blues groove.

Upbeat

Here are six more blues grooves. You'll hear each one played twice, followed by the next (with a measure of four "clicks" in between). Any of these could be extended to create a 12-bar blues.

Track 49

More Beats

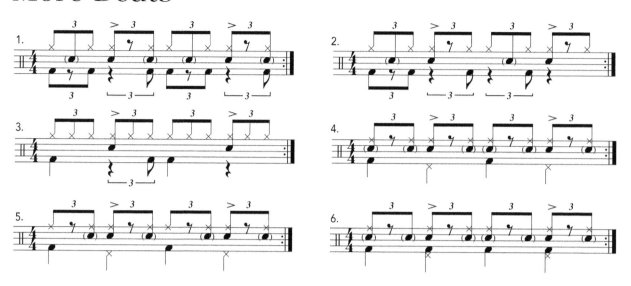

Ghostless Beats

The ghost notes are what make many of the previous beats cool, but to make them easier, we've taken them out for practice. Since #3 doesn't have any, and #4 and #5 would be the same without them, there's only four left.

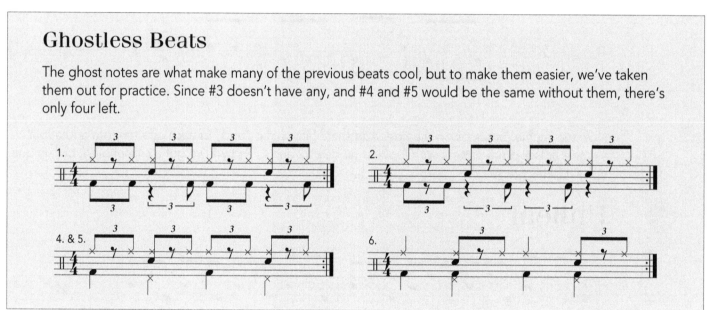

Following a Chart

On the next page, you'll see a basic blues chart, sometimes referred to as a "road map." Charts are useful for musicians playing a song together for the first time. They provide a quick overview of crucial aspects of the song—like its form, its chord progression, its style, tempo, etc.

For example, looking at this chart, you should recognize that the song is a 12-bar blues in three sections. The first section is a keyboard melody; the second, a guitar solo; the third, a repeat of the keyboard melody. The time signature (4/4) and the tempo and style (moderate shuffle) are also provided, giving you an idea of the overall feel of the song.

Interpreting a chart like this requires some creativity. The notation used—called **slash notation**—is very general. Each slash represents one beat in the current time signature and simply means that you should play something—anything—during that measure. Whatever you play, it would make sense that you continue in a similar style throughout the song. It would also make sense to highlight different sections by adding some variation—for example, playing on the hi-hat during the first and third sections, and switching to the ride for the guitar solo in the second section. (You would not, however, normally switch in the middle of a 12-bar section.)

There are purposely no drums on this track. Try all six examples from "More Beats," putting them into this chart and jamming with the band. You may want to insert a short fill at the end of each 12 bars to indicate that the form is about to start over or to end the song. Since this is a shuffle, it would make sense for your fills to be based on quarter notes or triplets (rather than straight eighths or sixteenth notes). Have fun playing these, and feel free to make up some of your own grooves to fit the song.

Track 50

Open Blues Jam

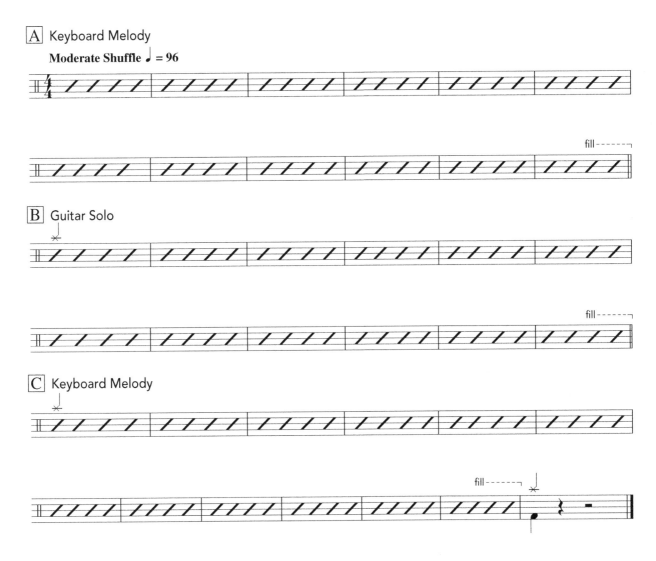

Just for a few ideas, here are some half-measure, shuffle-based fills. Try inserting any of these into your "Open Blues Jam."

Track 51

Half-Measure Fills

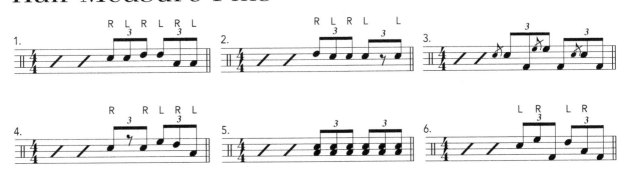

Modern Rock

Compared to early rock 'n' roll, modern rock—from the late '60s up to today—is more often straight eighth-note based rather than shuffled. The bass drum is generally busier, and the hi-hat (played with sticks) is used for the majority of the beats. Let's touch on a few of the dominant modern rock styles.

Hard Rock

Hard rock was strong from the late '60s through the '80s and could be described as loud, simple, and driving—with the help of the distorted guitar sound.

Keeping it simple doesn't have to be boring. Try "digging in" on this example using the half-open hi-hat sound.

Track 52

Solid

Accents on the Hi-Hat

A technique used to help drive the eighth-note pulse in modern rock is accenting beats 1, 2, 3, and 4 on the hi-hat. Typically, these accents are implied rather than notated.

Track 53

▶ Accent beats 1, 2, 3, and 4 on the hi-hat here.

Straight Forward

Sometimes it's very effective to play eighth notes on the floor tom instead of the hi-hat to help drive the beat along.

Track 54

Drivin'

Syncopated Sixteenths

The use of sixteenth notes in the next song is another example of *syncopation*, the placement of rhythmic accents on weak beats or weak portions of beats—in this case, the "e" of beat 3 on the snare, and the "a" of beats 2 and 3 on the bass drum.

Track 55

Syncopated

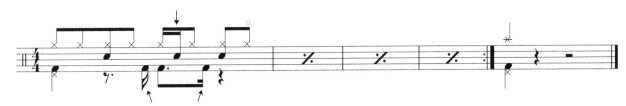

Alternative

In the early '90s, bands like Nirvana, Pearl Jam, and Soundgarden helped forge a new style of rock known as "alternative." Gone were the guitar solos of the '80s and in their place came a more stripped-down, textural approach to the instrument. Drums became a little busier, with straight eighth-note grooves giving way to frequent ghost notes and sixteenths.

This example is notated with the open hi-hat since the sound should be more than half-open. With your left foot on the hi-hat pedal, press down just enough so that the cymbals "sizzle" together when you're playing this very loudly. This one moves along pretty quickly; take it slowly to start with.

Track 56

Bashing

"Offbeat" makes good use of ghost notes. If playing these ghost notes is too difficult at first, take them out and practice the groove without them, playing the snare on beats 2 and 4 only.

Track 57

Offbeat

Now play straight sixteenth notes with your right stick on the hi-hat. Just line up the bass drum notes under the corresponding hi-hat notes to ensure the evenness. Notice when the open hi-hats occur and when to close them with your left foot.

Steady

Track 58

Sometimes, drummers use the crash cymbal to ride on. This technique has been around for quite some time, but it's been growing even more popular since the early '90s through today. Play on the edge of the crash cymbal, as you normally would, but continue, as in this case, with eighth notes. This creates a "shhh" sound, rather than the more defined sound of the closed hi-hat or even the ride.

It's common to accent the downbeats to help create the underlying quarter-note pulse. Try this on "Crash Riding."

Crash Riding

Track 59

Punk

"Back to the basics" describes what punk rock is all about. It's just louder, faster, and more abrasive than any other rock 'n' roll. It thrives on few chords and simple melodies. Some early punk bands included the Ramones and the Sex Pistols. Two of the more modern punk bands are Green Day and Rancid. These examples look simple, but it's all about playing fast with lots of endurance.

Fast

Track 60

This one really gets your bass drum foot going.

Track 61

Faster

The quarter-note pulse on the snare drum really drives this one along.

Track 62

Fastest

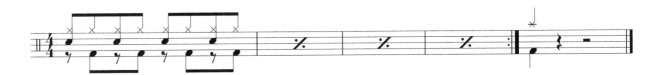

For a more "abrasive" sound, use the open hi-hat. Remember that you still want some "sizzle" to the hi-hat sound while you're playing it loud.

Track 63

Noise

► Start with the hi-hat and snare, then add the bass drum.

Take your time working out the syncopated bass drum part for this one before attempting to play it fast. Again, you might want to "lock in" on the hi-hat and snare pattern first.

Track 64

Out of Control

Metal

Metal (sometimes referred to as "heavy metal") is a form of rock music similar to hard rock, but technically more challenging. The songs are usually assembled around the guitar riff. The rhythms can be quite rigid with an almost military feel.

Track 65

Steel

For this example, the drum groove is very similar to the punk beats in the last section. The stylistic difference lies in the more technical guitar part.

Heavy

The difficulty in this example is playing the offbeat bass drum pattern. Notice that the last sixteenth bass drum note is played right into beat 1 of the repeat, making it even more challenging to play this one fast.

Defiance

► Here's another groove that rides on the crash cymbal.

Half Time

The next example, "Rigid," uses a half-time feel. Notice that the snare backbeat is on 3 instead of beats 2 and 4, which gives it this feel. Here is a comparison between the two.

Rigid

Harsh

Double Bass

Double bass drum playing started in the jazz and swing era but is now used mostly in modern rock and metal. Originally, "double bass" meant literally playing two bass drums—one with each foot. But with the advancement of bass drum pedals in the '80s, the double pedal became a more affordable way to play both beaters on one bass drum, eliminating the need to haul around an extra drum.

Having a double bass pedal isn't a necessity—many great drummers play without one. And you might not have one on your current kit. However, they do offer some advantages, allowing you to play faster on the bass drum by using both feet and making it easier to play for extended periods without tiring as quickly.

To give you a taste of what's possible, here are some popular double bass patterns. The left foot bass drum is notated on the lowest line of the staff. If you don't have a double pedal, try playing these grooves anyway (play both parts with just your right foot).

Track 70

Drivin' Eighths

This is similar to the last example, but it sounds a little less driving without playing the bass drum on 2 and 4.

Track 71

Less Driving

This is a classic double bass drum pattern—great for coordination and endurance. If you're practicing without a double bass pedal here, substitute your left foot on the hi-hat pedal. (In the right hand, instead of a half-open hi-hat, play the ride cymbal.)

Track 72

All Feet

Now try triplets with your feet. Notice beats 1 and 3 are played with the right foot, 2 and 4 with the left.

Track 73

Heavy Foot

Sometimes it's fun to play short bursts of bass drum notes. It's usually easier to play these faster since you can rest in between groups of notes.

Track 74

Speed Metal

Many times, it's possible to play grooves like the next one with only one foot, but using both feet allows you to make both sixteenth notes sound strong. You'll be able to play this faster, too.

Track 75

Broken Up

This has two quick bass drum notes just before beat 4. In case you're wondering, the three beams make them thirty-second notes.

Track 76

Swift Kick

► Thirty-second notes are twice as fast as sixteenth notes.

The Bounce

If you don't have a double bass pedal, you can still play many of the previous grooves—in particular, any with just two sixteenth kicks in a row (♪♪)—using a technique called the **bounce.** The bounce is based on the "heel up" approach to playing bass drum—using the ball of your foot on the pedal (heel up) and letting your whole leg come down, pivoting from the hip (as opposed to keeping the foot flat and using your ankle for this motion).

Try this: Begin playing as you normally would, with your heel up, but instead of letting the ball of your foot remain on the pedal as you bring your leg down, drop your heel first—letting it depress the pedal—and then roll your foot forward so that the ball of your foot plays a second note. It's sort of a two-part "rocking" motion: 1) heel, 2) ball.

hit #1: heel

hit #2: ball

You may want to imagine *lifting* up the ball of your foot as you strike with the heel, then *rolling forward.* (It's sort of a "skipping" motion.) It may also help to practice this with your shoes off so you can feel the pedal better.

Double bass is a great way to spice up your fills. The following examples use sixteenth notes and eighth-note triplets. Play each one twice with a measure of "clicks" in between. Make them flow as evenly as possible. (Try using the bounce for any fills that use just two kicks in a row.)

Track 77

Sixteenth Fills

Triplet Fills

Odd Time

So far we've covered 4/4, 3/4, and 12/8 time. The next song features a new time signature—6/4. There are six beats in a measure, and the quarter note receives one beat. This is considered "odd time." Other "popular" odd time signatures include 5/4 and 7/4.

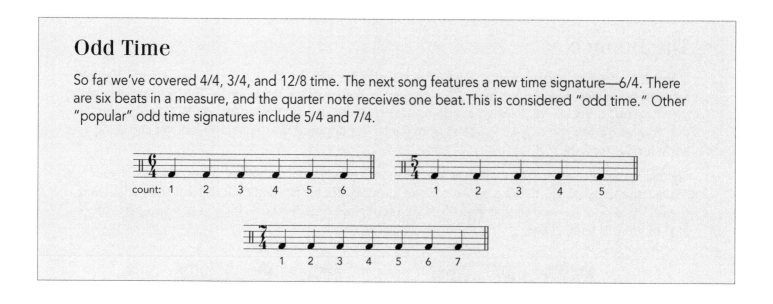

Be sure to count along as you play this one. Notice the time signature changes to 4/4 during the chorus, then back to 6/4 for the outro.

Track 78

Strangely Odd

► You'll hear six clicks on the count-in for this song.

Funk

In the late '60s, soul and rock began to mix to form a new style called "funk." James Brown and Sly Stone were the godfathers of funk; George Clinton and his bands Parliament/ Funkadelic represented the next breed of funksters.

Classic Funk

What makes funk beats so "funky" are the offbeat snare hits, ghost notes, and open hi-hats. Take your time with these; they can be quite tricky at first. Be aware of the accents and ghost notes. The dynamics between limbs make all the difference in the way these feel.

Everything happens here on beat 3.

Track 79

Slight Funk

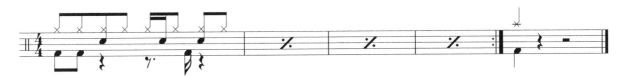

This fun example uses a very syncopated snare part. Even though it looks complicated, the hi-hat just plays straight eighth notes, and the snare notes fall in between. Play those accents!

Track 80

Funky

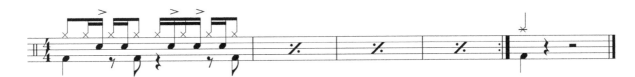

Funk beats often uses ghost notes, and this is a great example. The open hi-hats also make it interesting.

Track 81

Ghosting

Playing the last snare note on the "and" of 4 in the first measure creates a lull in the feeling of this groove. There are those ghost notes again!

Track 82

Freezing

Funk Rock

Funk rock, as the name implies, is a merger of "funk" and "rock" genres. The syncopated feel of the drums and the distorted guitar sound define this style.

The notes here are all simple, but they're not necessarily where you might expect them. Play this with conviction.

Quarter Funk

Modern rock beats tend to have quite a few bass drum kicks in them. When you mix this with funk, you wind up with quite a few notes to play!

Plenty of Notes

Funk Metal

Take the popping bass lines and syncopated rhythms of funk, combine them with the loud guitars and riffs of heavy metal, and you've got funk metal.

The syncopation happens more in the bass drum part of the following examples, rather than the snare, as in the classic funk beats.

Frenzy

Anger

Choppy

New Orleans

Many musical historians believe that all contemporary funk came from the New Orleans "second line" parade beat feel. The following are two basic second line patterns. Play each of these with alternating strokes on the snare drum.

In "Street March," play accents on the snare along with the bass drum rhythm.

Track 88

Street March

By changing the accents on the snare to beats 2 and 4, the feel of this similar pattern is now changed.

Track 89

New Orleans Backbeat

Disco

Disco originated from the groove-oriented sound of the '70s and funk. Disco is all about keeping a simple beat to dance to. A frequent sound is the open and closed hi-hat.

Try these popular disco patterns.

Track 90

Nightlife

Hip-Hop

Hip-hop is a type of funk that evolved from rap music. The shuffle indication in parentheses ( ) tells you to shuffle the sixteenth notes.

Track 91

Hip-Hop #1

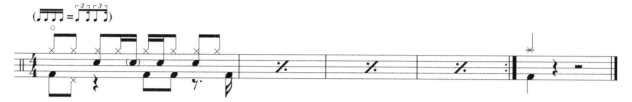

Hip-Hop #2

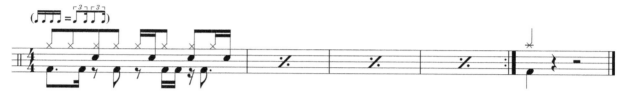

Track 92

Paradiddles

You may remember in Lesson 11 learning to play flams. These were an example of a **rudiment**—a specific sticking used to create a particular rhythmic pattern or effect. Another fun and useful rudiment is the "paradiddle."

A **single paradiddle** is a group of four evenly spaced notes (usually eighths or sixteenths) that are played with two alternating strokes followed by a double stroke. Often, you'll play two paradiddles in a row, as in the following example:

Practice this pattern until you can play it effortlessly and don't have to think about the sticking. Accenting the beginning of each four-note group makes it easier to hear the paradiddles. If it helps, try saying the name of the rudiment as you play it:

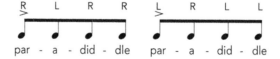

Now try adding the bass drum and playing your paradiddles faster.

42

Now try the **double paradiddle**. Just add two more alternating single strokes at the beginning of each single paradiddle, and you have double paraddidles.

Lastly, try the **triple paradiddle**. You guessed it: Add two alternating strokes to the beginning of each double paradiddle.

Practice all three of these until they become smooth and second nature to you. Another fun way to practice paradiddles is by playing them on the drumset using the toms too.

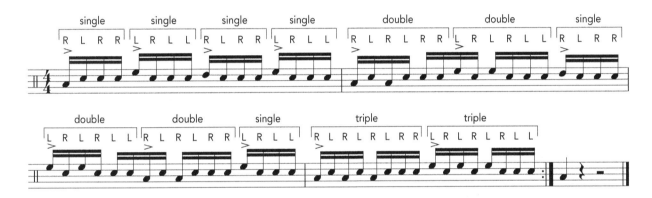

Here are a couple useful funk beats that use paradiddles. Keep your right stick on the hi-hat and your left on the snare. For starters, play all of the hi-hat and snare notes at the same volume. When you become more confident, play the ghost notes soft and the accents loud for the true feel of these grooves. These may look frightening at first—until you understand the concept.

Track 93

Single Paradiddle Funk

Double Paradiddle Funk

To close this lesson, we'll end with a short song incorporating paradiddles along with other funk beats and fills. Practice this song in sections first, before playing it all together.

Feeling Funky

Latin

Let's touch on some popular Latin rhythms. These are fun to play and will help build your coordination.

Samba

The samba is Brazilian in origin. It's a faster Latin style, often felt in "two" rather than "four."

Try playing this pattern on the bell of the ride cymbal (if you have a cowbell, use that as a substitute). Your left hand will play the cross-stick and reach up to then play the tom. After playing the tom, try to set the stick down quietly on the snare to play the cross-stick again.

Track 95

Samba Bell

If you find "Samba Bell" difficult, try practicing just the feet. This is the standard samba foot pattern:

Then try the same beat as above but with an eighth-note ride.

"Straight-Eighth Samba" features a popular samba clave on cross-stick. Remember the **clave**? It's a distinctive rhythm found in Latin music. Actually, it's more than just one rhythm—there are different clave patterns for different styles.

Track 96

Straight-Eighth Samba

► The clave (on cross-stick) should sound almost like a separate percussionist.

Bossa Nova

The bossa nova is another popular Brazilian rhythm that has been used by both rock and jazz bands. It's an outgrowth of the samba and usually has a slow to moderate 4/4 feel.

The cross-stick often imitates the sound of the clave rhythm. Try "The Bossa" and then "Reverse Bossa," which reverses the clave pattern played with the cross-stick.

The Bossa

Reverse Bossa

Mambo

Mambo is an Afro-Cuban dance style with a medium to up-tempo feel.

The mambo uses a broken right-hand pattern instead of steady eighth notes; this sounds great on the ride cymbal bell or on a cowbell. You may want to practice this groove starting with the left hand and feet parts first, adding the right-hand ride when you're comfortable.

Track 98

Let's Mambo

Cowbell

Cowbell is another percussion instrument you might want to add to your drumkit. It's a popular substitute for the ride cymbal and can also be used for solos or "breakdowns." In fact, if you have an extra pair of hands in your band, the cowbell is a great instrument on which to have the vocalist or another percussionist play the clave pattern.

Cha-Cha

Cha-cha is also Afro-Cuban in origin, and usually has a moderate 4/4 feel.

Eighth notes on the hi-hat, along with cross-stick quarter notes, help to drive this beat along.

Track 99

Cha-Cha, Anyone?

Changing Your Drumheads

If you've played through this book—or you've been playing drums for a while—you may notice that your drumheads are beginning to show some "wear and tear." Over time, drumheads stretch out and begin to lose their tone. If your drums came with white-coated heads and you can now see through them where you play a lot, or if they have dents, you may want to consider buying new heads. It's best to change all of your tom heads at the same time. The snare drum head might need to be changed more often since it's usually played much more.

What Type of Heads Do I Need?

Drumheads come in all different brands and types. If you bought your drumset new, typically it would come fitted with single-ply heads (because of their versatility). If you consider yourself mainly a rock drummer and play hard, you may want to try two-ply heads for your toms. Two-ply drumheads will last longer and produce a more muffled and deep tone. This applies to the bass drum as well. Before buying heads at your local drum store, talk to other, more experienced drummers about what they prefer.

To figure out what size drumheads you need, measure the diameter of each drum *inside* the metal hoop. You are actually measuring the drum shell. A typical five-piece drumset consists of a 22" bass drum, 14" snare, and 12", 13", and 16" toms. The measurements should always be rounded to the nearest inch. If you're not sure, take your drums along with you when buying heads, just to be safe.

Removal and Cleaning

Once you've decided on which heads to purchase, you'll now have to change them. If you're changing your tom heads, take the toms off of the drumset and place them on a carpeted floor in order from small to large. When removing the worn-out heads, take your drum key (the special tool that fits on the tension rods—the screws that tension down the drumhead on the shell) and turn counterclockwise on each rod to loosen the head. It's a good idea to turn each one just a little at a time—rather than loosening one rod completely before moving on to the next—to avoid uneven stress on the drum shell. This is especially true on snare drums, since they're usually tensioned the tightest. You don't need to remove the tension rods from the hoop; just let them dangle as you pull the head and hoop off the drum shell. At this point, you may want to remove any dust or foreign matter that possibly has accumulated inside the drum. As long as the head is off, take a screwdriver and lightly tighten the screws on the inside of the shell that may have loosened from the vibrations during playing. Be careful not to over-tighten the screws.

Installation and Tuning

Now take the new drumhead and place it on the drum. Separate the hoop from the old head and place it on the new head. Rethread the tension rods into the lugs with your fingers—being careful not to cross-thread—until they are finger-tight.

If your new head has a logo, start with the tension rod just to the right and tighten it a half turn. Now tighten the opposite rod the same. Then move to the next rod just to the right of where you first started and continue in the same fashion until you've tightened each a half turn. Now use the same pattern to give each rod another half turn all the way around the drum. Place your palm in the middle of the drum and put your other hand on top of that. Press down the head in the middle three or four times to stretch it in a little. You may hear a cracking sound (the drumhead resin settling) while doing this. This is normal. Take a drumstick and tap about an inch in from the hoop on the head at each tension point. Listen to the pitch of each. The object is to make them the same. Take your drum key and begin to tighten or loosen to make them match in pitch. If you are tuning the toms right now, you may be pretty close to the desired tension. Snare

drumheads are commonly tuned higher, so after matching the pitch at each rod, you may need to go around the drum again once or twice to reach the desired pitch.

Use this same procedure for all of the toms. After that point, you'll want to listen to the relationship in pitch between the different toms, so that no two drums are too close in pitch. If they are too close, using your drum key, repeat the same procedure to bring up or down the head of your choice. A head tuned quite low will feel flabby and make it more difficult to play fast fills, but tune mostly for the desired pitch you are looking for.

If you have toms with both top and bottom heads, you'll need to flip over the drum and tune those, too. Use the same tuning procedure on each bottom head, either matching the pitch to the top head or slightly higher. Don't be afraid to experiment. Tuning drums can be difficult and personal. It's not as easy as plugging a guitar into an electronic tuner. Take your time and practice this.